TOTALLY Human

Why We Look and Act the Way We Do

Written by **Cynthia Pratt Nicolson**

Illustrated by **Dianne Eastman**

Kids Can Press

For my family, a fine bunch of humans! — CPN   **For Paul and Emma — DE**

Acknowledgments

Research for this book took me to dozens of articles, books and websites on the fascinating science of human evolution. Two authors were particularly informative and inspiring. Paleontologist Neil Shubin, author of *Your Inner Fish: A Journey into the 3.5-Billion-Year History of the Human Body,* revealed the incredible physical connections we share with a line of ancestors stretching back to the earliest bacteria. Science journalist Hannah Holmes, author of *The Well-Dressed Ape: A Natural History of Myself,* supplied insight into the ancient reasons for our modern behavior. I would like to thank both authors for infusing their writing with an admirable sense of wonder about how we came to be the curious creatures we are today.

My gratitude also goes to Val Wyatt, whose excellent editorial ideas and suggestions have shaped this book from start to finish, and to Dianne Eastman, whose artwork adds fun to every page. Thanks as well to Karen Powers for her design work and to everyone at Kids Can Press for their commitment to producing high-quality books for children.

Kids Can Press acknowledges the financial support of the Government of Ontario, through the Ontario Media Development Corporation's Ontario Book Initiative; the Ontario Arts Council; the Canada Council for the Arts; and the Government of Canada, through the BPIDP, for our publishing activity.

Published in Canada by
Kids Can Press Ltd.
25 Dockside Drive
Toronto, ON M5A 0B5

Published in the U.S. by
Kids Can Press Ltd.
2250 Military Road
Tonawanda, NY 14150

www.kidscanpress.com

The artwork in this book was rendered in Adobe Photoshop CS3.
The text is set in Melior and Balboa.

Edited by Valerie Wyatt
Designed by Karen Powers

This book is smyth sewn casebound.
Manufactured in Altona, Manitoba, Canada, in 10/2011 by Friesens Corporation

CM 11 0 9 8 7 6 5 4 3

Image credits appear on page 40

Library and Archives Canada Cataloguing in Publication

Nicolson, Cynthia Pratt
    Totally human : why we look and act the way we do / written by Cynthia Pratt Nicolson ; illustrated by Dianne Eastman.

Includes bibliographical references.
ISBN 978-1-55453-569-9

1. Evolution (Biology)—Juvenile literature. 2. Evolutionary psychology—Juvenile literature. I. Eastman, Dianne II. Title.

QH367.1.N53 2011   j576.8   C2010-904769-9

Kids Can Press is a *Corus*™ Entertainment company

Contents

WHO are YOU?

You're special. You're unique. There's no one else in the universe exactly like you. But guess what? In many ways, you're just like the 6 billion other people on the planet. You do weird and wonderful things simply because you're human. Like other human beings, you look and act in certain ways — partly because of your experiences and partly because of your genes (coded instructions found in every cell of your body).

Your genes have quite a story to tell. You've inherited half your genes from your mother and half from your father. That's why you might hear that you have "your dad's eyebrows" or "your mom's big feet." Your parents, in turn, inherited genes from their parents, who inherited genes from their parents, and so on and so on and so on. In other words, you have a family tree of ancestors who have passed their genes along to you.

Your family tree stretches back to early humans who emerged on the plains of Africa about 175 000 years ago. Today, you still have some of their prehistoric looks and behaviors. But you've also inherited traits from the ancestors of early humans. These apelike species changed in appearance over millions of years as they went from swinging through trees to walking on two legs.

Going back still farther, your ancestors include early mammals, amphibians and fish. In fact, strange as it may seem, your family tree reaches back all the way to the first living things on Earth. Yes, you (and all other creatures) share genes with the bacteria (microscopic organisms) that sprang to life in our planet's steamy swamps about 3700 million years ago!

All of these ancestors — human, animal and even ancient bacteria — have contributed to the way you look and act. Some strategies that worked well long ago for them are still helpful today. Others seem puzzling and strange. In this book, we'll look at some of the odd things you (and all humans) do and ask "Why?"

Let's start (hic!) with a common problem (hic!) — yes, we're talking (hic!) about hiccups. Turn the page to (hic!) find out more.

Your inner chimpanzee

Although you share many genes with your ancestors, you also have genetic differences. That's because genes sometimes mutate (change) as they pass from generation to generation. Over billions of years, mutations have happened again and again. The amazing result? All the different species of life on Earth.

Although you are related to all animals, past and present, and share some of their genes, you are more closely related to some species than others. While you have only a few things in common with bacteria, you are closely related to all primates, a group that includes humans, chimpanzees, gorillas and monkeys. In fact, scientists have discovered that chimps, our closest living cousins, share an amazing 98 percent of our genes.

WHY do you get HICCUPS?

Think about the last time you had
hiccups. Did you hold your breath?
Gulp some water? What if nothing
worked and your hiccups lasted for
68 years? That's what happened to Charles
Osborne of Anthon, Iowa, who starting
hiccupping in 1922 and didn't stop until
1990, a year before his death. Luckily, most
hiccups stop after a minute or two. Still, they
can be annoying, embarrassing and sometimes
even painful.

It's hard to imagine that hiccups have a purpose,
but they do, as scientists have learned from
studying tadpoles (aka baby frogs). But before
we get to them, let's take a closer look at what
happens when you hiccup.

Hiccups begin with a spasm in the nerves that
control your breathing. The spasm makes you
breathe in quickly through your mouth. Almost
immediately, a tiny flap of tissue, called your
epiglottis, closes off your trachea (windpipe).
Hic! When the flap opens, you breathe normally
again — until the next spasm. Hic!

Back to tadpoles. Scientists knew that other
animals hiccupped, but they didn't know why.
Then they checked out tadpoles. These froglets
face a major challenge. As they mature, they stop
breathing through gills underwater and develop
lungs to breathe air. At one point, they have both
gills and lungs. To keep from breathing water into
their brand-new lungs, they hiccup.

Scientists tracked down the hiccup reflex and
discovered that it first appeared in the long-ago
ancestors of today's frogs. The hiccupping trait
was passed down through generation after
generation of amphibians. Over millions of years,
the genes for hiccupping also passed into reptiles
and then early mammals. Eventually, the
hiccupping mechanism ended up in modern
humans — and that includes you!

Ouch!

Ever touch a hot stove? If so, you probably
yanked your hand away even before your
brain had time to think, "Ouch! That
hurts!" The quick reaction of your arm
muscles is a reflex, an automatic action
beyond your control. Unlike throwing a
ball or washing your face, reflex actions
don't depend on messages from your
brain. Instead, they're triggered by
nerve signals that travel superfast from
your skin to your spinal cord to your
muscles.

You've inherited many reflexes from
your animal ancestors. As a new baby,
you instinctively grabbed onto fingers
and sucked anything that went in
your mouth. For millions of years,
these built-in actions have helped
young primates cling to adults and
drink their mothers' milk. You've
outgrown your newborn reflexes,
but you still have others, such as
blinking automatically to protect
your eyes when anything comes near
your face.

Some reflexes, like hiccupping, no
longer serve a purpose for humans.
Others, like pulling away from pain,
play an important role: keeping you
safe and sound.

WHY do you crave JUNK food?

Can you eat just one potato chip? Probably not. If you're like most people, you reach for another chip and then another, until the bag is empty.

You also probably know that junk food is bad for your health. Potato chips, loaded with salt and fat, can lead to high blood pressure and clogged arteries. And other junk food, such as sugary soft drinks and candy bars, rot your teeth and pile on extra weight. So if junk foods are so bad for you, why, oh why, do they taste so good?

To answer that question, let's step back in time to the days of your cave-dwelling ancestors. For those folks, finding food was a big deal. No trip to the kitchen or fast-food restaurant for them. Tracking an antelope or searching for edible plants could take all day. As an early human, you would have had to get used to a grumbling, hungry tummy.

When you were lucky enough to find something sugary (like ripe berries) or fatty (like a juicy mastodon), it made sense to gobble as much as possible. Your body told you to stock up. After all, who knew where the next meal was coming from? Early humans with strong appetites tended to survive and have more children. The powerful longing for sugar, salt and fat was passed along in their genes.

But times have changed. Today, a quick lunch of a burger, fries and a milkshake can add up to 84 g (3 oz.) of fat and 148 g (5 oz.) of sugar — more than enough for the whole day. Part of your brain tells you that's way too much, but another part sends the ancient message — eat lots now because you might not get another chance. Please pass the chips!

Don't forget to EAT!

Over millions of years, animals have developed strategies to make sure they eat enough to survive. Some of those strategies are built into your body.

When your rumbling tummy signals hunger, your brain sends out chemical messengers, called hormones, that travel through your bloodstream to all parts of your body. One hormone, ghrelin, increases your feeling of being hungry. Another hormone, leptin, carries the message that you've had enough. Unfortunately, it takes a while for your brain to "get" those hormone signals and act on them. So you might keep eating long after your leptin tells you it's time to quit.

Me want chips!

WHY do you BURP and FART?

Whew!

Have you ever pretended that a fart or burp came from someone else?
That trick wouldn't have worked for Paul Hunn of England. In 2008, he recorded the world's loudest burp. At 107.1 decibels, his burp was louder than a chainsaw just a meter (yard) from your ear!

Burps and farts might not be polite, but they are a regular part of your digestive system. Like some of your earliest animal ancestors, such as worms and fish, you have a body that is a "tube within a tube." Food goes in one end (your mouth), and wastes come out the other (your anus). Two rings of muscle called sphincters keep things from spilling out at either end. And those two sphincters play a big role in burps and farts.

The "tube within a tube" arrangement has plenty of advantages. It keeps food separate from wastes. And it lets sensory organs, such as eyes and ears, cluster around the food entry — a handy arrangement for a hungry creature looking for food. It's no wonder that thousands of animal species, from leeches to leopards, have this same basic layout.

But back to those burps and farts. When you eat, food is broken up and digested, first in your mouth and next in your stomach. Sometimes the reaction between your stomach juices and the food produces gases. If the pressure becomes too great, gases escape back up your esophagus (eating tube). Before coming out your mouth, the gases pass through the esophageal sphincter. Vibrations of the sphincter, not your voice box, make those funny burping sounds. Depending on how much gas there is and how quickly it passes through the sphincter, the result can be a quiet little burp or a loud BELCH!

Farther down your digestive track, your intestines are full of bacteria. The bacteria break down food, some of which is absorbed into your bloodstream so that it can go to all parts of your body. Some is packed into solid waste. Depending on what you've eaten and the bacteria in your gut, gases are also produced. Again, if the pressure becomes too great, they escape. This time, it's your anal sphincter that vibrates and makes the farting sound. Oops! It wasn't me! Honest!

Bacteria buddies

Bacteria can be a nuisance when they produce smelly farts or make your feet stink. And harmful types of bacteria cause disease and infection. But you couldn't live without the trillions of helpful bacteria that call your body home. In a process called symbiosis, bacteria have lived in and on the bodies of animals for millions of years.

Sharing a body has major advantages for you and your tiny guests. The bacteria help digest certain foods and keep harmful types of bacteria under control, which is good for you. And the good bacteria get a comfortable, warm home with plenty of nutrients. Strange as it seems, it's a win–win situation all around.

WHY do you THROW UP?

Yech!

Eeeww! Throwing up, vomiting, puking, barfing, tossing your cookies, emesis — no matter what you call it, it's gross. But vomiting is also a useful adaptation that goes way back in animal history.

Vomiting developed as a way of getting poisons out of a body before they could be absorbed into the bloodstream. This was useful for your early animal ancestors, who had no refrigerators or "best before" dates on their food. Vomiting could prevent death if a meal accidentally included poisonous plants or rotten meat.

Throwing up is controlled by a part of your brain called the medulla. When the medulla senses toxins in your body, it sends out signals that say, "Get rid of that food!" Muscles begin to contract throughout your body, including your stomach and the rest of your digestive tract. Repeated waves of contractions push the contents of your stomach out through your mouth. Because your stomach contains acid to help digest your food, the vomit has a bitter taste that makes the sensation even worse.

Ever wonder why your vomit sometimes contains little chunks of orange stuff even if you haven't eaten anything orange colored? These are bits of your stomach lining, torn off by the squeezing action. That may sound bad, but next time you throw up consider the sea cucumber. This soft-bodied ocean animal is the ultimate vomiter. When scared, a sea cucumber ejects not only recently eaten food but its entire stomach and other internal organs. Now that's losing your lunch!

Yikes! Run!

Spaced out

Have you ever felt your stomach lurch when an elevator drops quickly? If so, you have an idea of how astronauts feel when they begin learning to live in zero gravity. Astronauts train in a special plane that flies high above Earth and then drops suddenly, which gives them the weird, dizzying feeling of being weightless. Although the astronauts are having a truly modern experience, their bodies react in an ancient way — they get nauseated. Long ago, this sensation probably meant you had eaten something rotten or picked up some very bad germs. The safest way to react? Throw up, of course! No wonder crews gave the training plane its disgusting nickname: the Vomit Comet.

WHY do you SHAKE when you're SCARED?

Your heart is pounding. Your hands shake. Your breathing speeds up. What's wrong? You're scared, and your body is preparing to fight an attacker — or run away, FAST! It's an ancient response called "fight or flight."

Instant readiness for combat or a quick escape made lots of sense for long-ago humans, who might meet a herd of angry elephants or stampeding rhinos out on the African plains. The strategy was successful — fight-or-flighters had a better chance of surviving, and the response got passed along through their genes to you. So, even though you aren't likely to run into any snarling lions, your body still reacts to a big fright by prepping for all-out action.

Several things happen when a scare triggers your fight-or-flight response. First, a chemical called adrenaline floods through your body. Adrenaline is like a siren going off, carrying alarm signals to all your cells. Different parts of your body respond in different ways.

Adrenaline makes your heart pump harder and faster to send oxygen-carrying blood to your muscles, where the oxygen can boost muscle performance. Your breathing speeds up to replenish the oxygen supplies. Your eyes open wide, and your pupils enlarge to let in more light — so you can see things (including danger) more clearly. You might even get a stomachache or sudden cramp as your digestion shuts down to save energy.

Adrenaline also puts your arm and leg muscles on high alert. Your nerves fire off rapid signals telling the muscles, "Move! Move!" Muscle fibers contract and start to twitch. Your hands shake, and your knees feel wobbly. Yikes!

But what if your fears are caused by having to give a speech to your class? Obviously, you don't want to be trembling and gasping for air. It's time to take some deep, slow breaths, relax your muscles and remind yourself that, at least for now, you aren't about to be eaten by hyenas. Phew!

Scared strong

Adrenaline can make you shake, but it's also been credited for some amazing feats of strength and bravery. When 18-year-old Kyle Holtrust was pinned under a car in Tucson, Arizona, passerby Tom Boyle rushed over and lifted the vehicle while someone pulled Kyle to safety.

In Ivujivik, Quebec, Lydia Angyiou saw a large polar bear closing in on her son and another boy. Lydia wrestled the bear long enough for the boys to run to a neighbor for help.

WHY do you have two EARS?

Hey! What's that? Next time you're surprised by a strange sound, notice what you do with your head. Chances are you turn or tilt it. You might even hold a hand behind one ear. What's going on?

When you hear an unexpected noise, such as a loud *grrr!,* your brain automatically tries to figure out where the sound is coming from. Because your ears are on opposite sides of your head, the sound reaches one ear slightly before the other. It also seems a tiny bit louder on one side. Your brain uses these clues to pinpoint the source of the growling. You might turn or tilt your head to reposition your ears and check your first impression. An angry dog (or wolf!) on your left? Time to head right — fast! Being able to quickly find the source of a sound, whether predator or prey, was essential for your animal ancestors.

So, your two ears help you locate sounds, but what's with the fleshy flaps? Wouldn't simple holes in your head work just as well? Not really. Your outer ears, called pinnae, help collect sound waves. They're like tiny satellite dishes stuck onto the sides of your head — they funnel the sound waves into your inner ear, where signals are transmitted to your brain. When you cup a hand around an ear, you're simply extending your ear flaps to make them even better sound gatherers.

If ear flaps are so helpful, why aren't yours even larger? After all, some animals, such as African elephants and desert foxes, have ears that are bigger than their heads. These jumbo ears help their owners hear better — and get rid of excess heat — but they come at a cost. Growing enormous body parts takes lots of food and energy. Because your early human ancestors depended more on seeing than hearing, they didn't need huge ears and developed the medium-sized ears you have today. You could say you've got perfect pinnae!

WHY are you swayed by SMELLS?

Most of the time, you don't think much about the smells around you. You get used to the scent of your own house or classroom. But when a new smell comes along, suddenly your nose is on patrol. Whether you've picked up a delightful aroma (cookies baking) or a horrible stench (rancid leftovers), you can't help but notice it.

For many animals, smell is the best way to learn about the environment. Because you're human, you use your eyes more than your nose, but scents still trigger strong reactions in an ancient part of your brain, two almond-shaped lumps called the amygdalae.

Smelling developed as a good way to detect food, a mate or a predator. Your earliest ancestors lived in the sea and, like modern fish, they were highly sensitive to scent molecules spread through the water. Sharks, for instance, can detect a tiny drop of blood from over 100 meters (109 yards) away. Later, when animals moved onto land, they picked up smells dispersed through the air. Your nostrils can pick up even a few molecules of a strong scent in a large roomful of air. Then your nerves send the information to your brain. That's where the decision is made — is this smell good or bad? Helpful or harmful?

Your ancient ancestors depended on their noses. A strong sense of smell meant a strong ability to survive. Today, our sense of smell is not as crucial — our eyes are our main information gatherers — but our amygdalae still react to smells. Interestingly, the amygdalae also store memories and emotions. Just one whiff of a forgotten smell, such as your grandmother's perfume, can bring back powerful feelings from the past.

WHY do your EYES face forward?

Here's a quick experiment. Extend your arms straight out in front of you, at shoulder height. Close one eye and slowly bring the tips of your pointer fingers together. Now do the same thing with both eyes open. Why is it so much easier with two eyes than with one?

When you use both eyes, you can judge distances much more accurately. Your eyes face forward, and the small space between them gives you two slightly different views of the world. Your brain combines the information from left and right to create a single, three-dimensional image. Touching fingertips becomes a snap.

Of course, your ancient human ancestors didn't sit around staring at their fingers. They used their distance-judging ability for important jobs, such as bringing down dinner with a rock or spear. Even earlier ancestors may have needed forward-facing vision as they swung from branch to branch in the treetops. How far is that branch? A little farther than you thought? Oops!

Forward-facing eyes are a trait you share with wolves, cougars, hawks and bears. As you might have noticed, all of these animals are predators who use vision to nab their prey. Animals with eyes on the sides of their heads — such as rabbits and fish — typically need to be on the lookout to avoid being attacked. They can see all around but lack predators' ability to judge distances. Chameleons (a type of lizard) have the best of both worlds. Their bulging eyes swivel independently to look up, down, sideways and forward. With two eyes trained straight ahead, a chameleon can locate a tasty insect and then extend its long, sticky tongue. Zap!

18

WHY do you SEE COLORS?

Would you rather be a bat or a butterfly? If you like seeing the world in color, a butterfly is a better choice. To a bat, everything looks black, white or gray. Many butterflies, on the other hand, can see more colors than a human.

Different animal species have evolved different levels of color vision, depending on their lifestyles. Animals that hunt at night, such as bats and owls, don't depend on color to distinguish their prey. Shades of gray are all they see. Other animals, including butterflies and humans, are active in the daytime. They see the world in glorious color.

Scientists think color vision was a lifesaving advantage for your apelike ancestors. When gathering food, they could quickly distinguish ripe red berries from sour (and possibly toxic) green ones. Striding across the African plains, they could spot a poisonous orange snake slithering toward them through the long, green grass. Seeing in color is more than just a pleasant way to view your surroundings. It's an important part of your ancient survival tool kit.

Silly symbols like these ;-) are called emoticons.

They were invented to solve a problem. People were receiving e-mails — and getting mad. They couldn't tell if the person writing to them was joking or serious, cheerful or angry. Without a face to look at, the message was often misinterpreted.

Your face constantly sends out signals to the people around you. At the same time, you pick up signals from their faces. All around the world, people share the seven basic emotions — anger, sadness, joy, contempt, disgust, fear and surprise — with the same expressions. It's a silent language that all humans know.

Being able to "read" each other's faces means you and your family, friends, teachers and even strangers can get along more easily. Where does this ability come from? Scientists figure you're born with it. As a tiny baby, you stared intently at anything face-like — even two dots above a straight line.

Around one month of age, you returned a toothless grin when someone smiled at you. When you felt sad, you pulled down the corners of your mouth until someone picked you up — or maybe changed your diaper.

Long ago, your apelike ancestors also used facial expressions to communicate. A scowl might mean, "Back off!" while a fearful expression said, "Don't attack me!" Being able to read faces made it possible to understand other people better and live harmoniously with them. And as part of a group, your ancestors had a much better chance of survival than going it alone.

Not sure about the value of a smile? Consider people with a rare disorder called Moebius syndrome. They can't grin, frown or even show surprise. Why? Because they were born without the nerves needed to trigger movement in their face muscles.

Dr. Ron Zuker at the Hospital for Sick Children in Toronto wanted to help people with Moebius syndrome. He figured out a way to transplant small pieces of muscle from their thighs to their cheeks. After surgery, Dr. Zuker's patients practice using the new muscles to pull up the corners of their mouths. Their hard-won smiles? Priceless!

Smile power

You smile because you *feel* happy, right? Usually. But the reverse can also be true — sometimes smiling can *make* you feel happy. Researchers studied people's reactions to funny cartoons. Some of the people were asked to hold a pen in their teeth, which gave them a smiling face.

Others held a pen with their lips, giving them a disappointed expression. The result? People who held a pen in their teeth (the smilers) found the cartoons much more amusing. In other words, the expression on your face can affect your feelings. Try smiling right now. How do you feel?

WHY do you LAUGH?

What does a pig put on a cut?

Oink-ment!

Why does Mount Everest hear so well?

It's covered with mountain-eers!

Did you laugh out loud at these goofy jokes?

Probably not, if you're reading this book to yourself. Share a joke, though, and the chance of a chuckle goes way up. But you don't need jokes to prompt a giggle. Strange as it seems, most laughter has nothing to do with things being funny.

Scientists have studied laughter — seriously! They've found that people laugh most during ordinary conversations. For some reason, comments like "How's it going?" and "See you later!" are often accompanied by laughter. And it's the speaker, rather than the listener, who usually does the most chuckling. What's going on?

Laughter, like smiling and crying, is a social signal. It probably evolved from the open-mouthed panting your apelike ancestors did while they were playing. This panting told the playmate that the roughhousing was all in fun. Today, you laugh during a conversation to signal that you are feeling friendly — not dangerous or threatening.

Laughter connects you with other people. A shared laugh says, "We're all part of the same gang," and that feels good. So laughter brings you into a group. And for millions of years, being part of a group has been the best way to survive.

WHY do you CRY?

What's one thing that you do that no other animal does? *Waaaa!* It's crying. Other animals make sad noises — they may moan or howl, for instance — but none, not even our closest living relatives, the chimpanzees, shed tears of emotion like we do.

You have three different kinds of tears. Basal tears keep your eyes moist. Reflex tears well up when your eyes are irritated, such as when you chop an onion. Other animals have both of these types of tears. But the third type, the tears of emotion that you get when you are sad or super happy, are not found in any other species.

What is the purpose of emotional tears? Scientists have found that these tears contain higher-than-normal levels of chemicals that make your body feel less stressed. Tears may be a way of releasing these chemicals to calm you down.

Tears running down your face is another way — besides howling and moaning — of showing your emotions. People who see someone crying often feel empathy — the ability to understand and care about another person's feelings. This ability helped your ancestors live together in close communities. And that helped them survive — even though many other animals were stronger or faster, early humans found strength in numbers. Crying (and the empathy it produced in others) helped early humans bond together.

WHY do you feel TICKLISH?

HEE HEE HEE HEE HEE HEE HEE HEE HEE HEE HEE HEE HEE HEE HEE HEE HEE HEE HEE HEE HEE HEE HEE HEE HEE HEE HEE HEE HEE HEE HEE HEE HEE HEE HEE HEE HEE HEE HEE HEE

HEE HEE HEE HEE HEE HEE HEE HEE HEE HEE HEE HEE HEE HEE HEE HEE HEE HEE HEE HEE HEE HEE HEE HEE HEE HEE HEE HEE HEE HEE HEE HEE HEE HEE HEE HEE HEE HEE HEE HEE

24

When you were a baby, you probably chortled when someone lightly stroked your chubby feet. As you got older, you laughed when one of your parents, or an older brother or sister, grabbed and tickled you. The underarms, waist, ribs and feet are especially ticklish for most people, and a light tickle in these areas can be almost painful if you are supersensitive. Even so, you would probably laugh anyway.

Why do you laugh when you're tickled? Tickling is a mock attack. When someone grabs you, keeps you from moving and then tickles you, there's a sudden "Oh no!" Then, as your brain realizes, "Hey, this is just for fun," there's a release of tension, and you laugh in relief.

Why can't you tickle yourself? Because there's no way to fool yourself into thinking the attack is real. Maybe that's also why children have a hard time tickling adults. Kids just aren't scary enough.

Tickling probably started long ago with our apelike relatives, and the behavior got passed along. Today's chimpanzees, our closest living relatives, enjoy tickling and being tickled. Chimp mothers pretend to bite their babies and tickle them while making a face that says, "I'm just playing." Researchers have also tickled chimpanzees the way they would another human to see what happens. The chimps pant with their mouths open — their form of laughter.

Tickling seems like simple silliness. But scientists believe it has an important function. All that touching and laughing builds up bonds among friends and family. When it came time to hunt a mastodon or build a shelter in the trees, early humans who had a strong web of close relationships were more likely to work well together and succeed.

Tickle me, Ratso

American scientist Jaak Panksepp found his laboratory rats liked being tickled. They would even run over when he put his hand into their cages. The rats seemed to enjoy the tickles in silence, but when Panksepp analyzed sound recordings of the tickling episodes, he made a discovery. The rats were making chirps too high pitched for humans to hear. It seems the tickling produced lots of rodent-style giggling.

WHY do you like MUSIC?

Imagine you're watching a movie in which two men are fishing in a small rowboat. As they laugh and chat, you happily munch your popcorn. Then, for some reason, you start to feel nervous. Something terrible is going to happen! The men in the rowboat are still laughing, but you feel more and more anxious. What's going on?

The answer lies in the movie's soundtrack. While you watched, the background music switched from light and cheery to dark and menacing. It psyched you up for the next scene, where — YIKES! — the boat is attacked by a huge, toothy shark!

Moviemakers know that music has power. It "speaks" directly to your emotions without using words. Around the world, people use melody and rhythm to share their feelings and influence the emotions of others. Rock bands, for instance, use pounding beats to energize their audiences. Soccer fans sing loudly to cheer on their teams. In centuries past, Celtic musicians inspired their warriors and scared (or, at least, puzzled) their enemies with the weird wailing of bagpipes.

But music isn't always exciting and stimulating. In fact, the very first music was probably just the opposite. Researchers believe that music began when early primates murmured comforting sounds to their offspring while rocking them in hairy hugs. Over millions of years, the soothing sounds developed into the lullabies today's parents sing to put their babies to sleep.

Rock, country, classical or jazz — music brings people together. Even when you tune in alone on your iPod, you are sharing melodies and rhythms that others have created and enjoyed. From the mountaintops of Tibet to the street corners of New York, music helps humans communicate and also binds them together. Who knows? One day, music may even help us communicate with aliens. Recordings of music were sent into space on the *Voyager 1* spacecraft in 1977 in the hope that an alien civilization might one day think, "Hey, those Earthlings sound cool! We should get to know them." No wonder music is called "the universal language."

Boppin' back in time

Pop (for "popular") music echoes around the world and way back in time. The first instruments were probably invented when your early human ancestors got the beat by pounding sticks on hollow logs or rapping two stones together. No one knows when other instruments appeared, but archaeologists have unearthed whistles and flutes made from bird bones about 37 000 years ago. The first known "recorded" song was created over 4000 years ago in the ancient land of Sumer in the Middle East. The song, a love ballad, was written on a clay tablet in the newly invented cuneiform script.

WHY do you TALK?

You don't have pointy fangs like a panther, sharp eyes like an eagle or speedy legs like a gazelle. Let's face it, compared to many other animals, you are a small, slow weakling. But there's good news. Over hundreds of thousands of years, your species has developed a secret weapon — language.

No one knows exactly when humans first started speaking, but everyone agrees that language gave our species a huge advantage. Language helped early humans tell each other about sources of food and water. It let people talk about the past — and make plans for the future. With words, they could plan hunts and use teamwork to capture animals much larger and faster than themselves.

The ability to learn language seems to be built into your brain. In fact, you started learning to talk even before you were born. In a recent study, researchers in Europe found that two-day-old babies made different crying sounds depending on whether their mothers spoke French or German. The scientists believe the babies learned the rising and falling pitches of their mothers' speech while they were still in the womb. When they started crying, they tended to match those patterns.

You probably started making babbling sounds when you were about three months old and spoke real words after your first birthday. By the time you were four, you were speaking your "mother tongue" more or less fluently. You had already learned hundreds of words and the rules for putting them together to make sense. This incredible feat leads some scientists to conclude that the human brain is specially wired for language.

With language, early humans were able to think of things beyond what was directly in front of them. Storytelling became a way of explaining the world and remembering important information. Knowledge and survival skills could be passed from parents to children. Disputes could (sometimes) be settled with words instead of weapons. Language — and the teamwork it allows — made it possible for humans to become the dominant species on the planet. Not bad for a weakling!

Two-legged talkers

About 4 million years ago, your apelike ancestors began to walk on two legs instead of four. This was a major milestone on the journey to becoming human. Hands and arms were now free for gesturing and carrying. Long legs and a flexible spine made long-distance running a breeze. Throats and jaws (transformed in shape and size) could now manage the controlled breathing needed for making different sounds. With brains that had enlarged in pace with all these other changes, your ancestors were ready for a huge leap forward. Roughly 100 000 years ago, they began to speak.

WHY do you use your RIGHT (or LEFT) hand more?

Very handy!

Place the palms of your hands together. Your hands are mirror versions of each other, right? Now pick up a pen and write your name with one hand, then the other. Do your hands still seem so similar? Probably not.

If you're like most people, you have a dominant hand, and for eight or nine people out of ten, it's the right hand. Some rare people are ambidextrous — they can use either hand equally well. But even children who start out being ambidextrous usually develop a dominant hand by the time they are five.

Skillful hands (with opposable thumbs that can touch every finger) gave early humans a major advantage over their apelike ancestors. But why should one hand be more capable than the other? Although the answer isn't fully understood, scientists have some clues.

For one thing, it isn't only one hand that outshines the other. You probably also have an ear, an eye and a foot that are stronger than their partners. The lopsidedness of your body starts in your genes; it's something you're born with. But it's also reinforced every time you use one side of your body more. If you always kick a soccer ball with your left foot, for instance, that foot (and leg) will become more skillful. What starts as a small difference may become a major imbalance.

Another clue comes from your brain. Like the rest of your body, this soft, beige lump has two distinct sides. The right and left halves, called hemispheres, look like mirror images of each other, but they are not identical. Generally speaking, your left hemisphere is more active when you are speaking, doing math or solving a logical problem. It controls the right side of your body. Your brain's right hemisphere is more likely to help you with such things as seeing shapes, recognizing faces and appreciating music. It controls the left side of your body. A band of brain tissue, called the corpus callosum, joins the two hemispheres and enables them to interact in complex ways.

Some scientists believe that focusing attention on one hand may allow your brain to work more efficiently. In an emergency, for instance, you don't hesitate while deciding which hand to use. When your ancestors were under attack, a quick response — grabbing a stick or throwing a rock — meant success or failure, life or death. You could say handedness was handy!

A dominant flipper?

Humans aren't alone when it comes to favoring one side of the body. In 2001, researchers filmed walruses feeding underwater off the coast of Greenland. The enormous sea creatures use their flippers to dig up clams and mussels from the ocean floor. Surprisingly, one flipper — the right — is used almost all the time. In another study, scientists at the Yerkes National Primate Research Center in Atlanta, Georgia, made a similar discovery with chimpanzees. Whether greeting each other, making threats or stretching out an open palm for food, most chimps use their right hand more often than their left.

WHY do you REMEMBER?

You hear loud screams and wild laughter.
The smoky smell of hot dogs and onions wafts through the air. Happy strangers bump into you, and cotton candy melts on your tongue. Where are you? That's right — at an amusement park. Now fast forward to the next day. You want to tell a friend about being completely soaked in the final plunge of the log ride. How do you retrieve the memory?

Your brain is made up of over 100 billion cells called neurons, connected to each other in an incredibly complicated web. Each link between neurons is called a synapse. When you have an experience, your nerves conduct electrical impulses to your brain from your eyes, ears, skin and other parts of your body. Your brain processes these signals by strengthening existing synapses and creating new ones. In effect, your memories are collections of synapses in your brain. Some memories — like being submerged in the log ride — might stay with you for the rest of your life. Others, probably less important or meaningful, will quickly disappear.

You inherited your good memory from your early human ancestors. With the ability to remember a sequence of actions, they could learn useful skills, such as toolmaking and basket weaving. Recalling words and stories made it possible to transmit knowledge to their children. And, perhaps most important, a strong memory gave your ancestors the tremendous advantage of recognizing trusted friends. Long before Facebook, they could excel at social networking!

WHY do you YAWN?

Ever notice that when you yawn, other people around you start to yawn, too? Scientists aren't sure why people yawn, but they do have some theories. Yawning may be a way of helping your body take in more oxygen and wake up if you're feeling sleepy. However, people also yawn when they're bored or nervous. But the big question is: Why is yawning so contagious?

Yawns are most often passed between close friends. Strangers aren't as likely to catch the urge. And adults don't pick up yawns from kids as easily as kids spread yawns among themselves. All these things tell us that yawns are about relationships between people. Try it yourself. Yawn at the dinner table and see who yawns with you — your parents or your siblings?

Like many other human behaviors, yawning may be a way for people to bond with each other. You're tired? Me too! Yawns might also have helped coordinate sleeping times. When your cave-dwelling ancestors sat around an open fire, one big yawn could trigger several more. Without clocks or watches, yawning might have been the signal that told everyone "It's time for bed."

WHY do you SLEEP?

Grumpy. Dopey. Sleepy. No, we're not talking about Snow White's pals. These words probably describe you when you don't get enough sleep.

Humans vary in the amount of sleep they need — from 18 hours a day as young babies to eight or less as adults. Kids your age function best with at least nine hours of sleep a night.

What's the big deal about sleep? Think about a computer. To save energy, it automatically "goes to sleep" when it's not being used. Some scientists think that's also the main reason humans sleep. Being awake and active all the time requires a lot more food to fuel muscles and brains. While this might not be a problem for you, your ancestors had to work hard for every meal. Saving energy was a definite advantage.

The need for sleep may have had another use long ago. Sleep might also have helped your ancestors avoid predators. Early humans probably searched out caves and other tucked-away places to hide while they slept. They increased their chances of survival by making it harder for hungry animals to find them.

Finally, sleep gives your body a chance to grow and repair itself. When you've had a good night's sleep, you're ready for the day ahead. With so many benefits to provide, it's not surprising that the need to sleep is built into your genes.

Wakey, wakey. Rise and shine.

WHY do you PLAY?

If you've ever watched a pair of kittens, you know they tumble and wrestle, hop towards one another and away again, dash across the furniture and even up the curtains, if they're not stopped. Cute, yes, but there's a serious purpose behind all that fooling around. When they play, kittens are practicing the hunting and stalking skills their wild ancestors needed for survival.

Active play, the kind that kittens do, makes bodies physically stronger. When you play, you develop skills like jumping, climbing and throwing. You improve your balance and hand-eye coordination. Skills like these were essential to your tree-dwelling ancestors. (Ever wonder why so many playgrounds have "monkey bars"?) But there's a lot more to play than just swinging from branches.

Scientists who have studied animal behavior say that play gives you a chance to try out actions without bad consequences if things go wrong. During games, for example, you learn to get along with other people. You find out how to share and take turns, skills that you'll need as you grow up. Make-believe play gives you a chance to solve problems and try out adult roles.

Young animals, including humans, enjoy play. It's a trait that you've inherited in your genes. That's a good thing because fooling around as a youngster prepares you for life later on. Strange as it seems, play is a chance for serious learning. It's definitely more than just fun and games.

WHY do you love PETS?

Watch a dog wag its tail. What could be happier? Well, maybe the human who is hugging that dog. If you have a pet, or a friend with a pet, you know that animals bring joy into many people's lives.

When did we start welcoming other species into our homes? Probably during the last Ice Age, about 100 000 years ago. As your human ancestors struggled to survive in the ice and snow, they needed to be alert to the presence of other animals. A giant sloth would make a tasty meal. A saber-toothed tiger could make a meal out of you. Having a pet might have warned ancient people when other animals were nearby.

Although no one is sure exactly how it happened, dogs descended from wolves to become the very first pets. Hungry wolves may have approached human camps, scavenging for scraps of food. Some, less fearful than others, may have stayed around the edges of the camp, slowly becoming more and more dependent on people. Or perhaps a group of children found an orphaned pup and carried it home, snuggling their faces in its soft fur.

Humans gradually tamed the wild visitors. They selected the friendliest individuals for pets and then kept their offspring. This went on for generation after generation. Eventually, by about 15 000 years ago, these early pets were no longer wolves. They had become domesticated dogs. It was the start of a long-lasting friendship.

Cats were also brought into human homes. The purring creatures you know today developed from their wild ancestors about 10 000 years ago. Like dogs, cats were tamed with the help of humans who selected individuals to breed.

Recent studies have shown that pets can reduce their owners' stress and help hospital patients feel less pain. Scientists tell us that patting a dog or cat can raise your level of oxytocin, a hormone that brings feelings of pleasure. Of course, your ancient ancestors knew nothing of oxytocin or stress levels. They just knew there was something special about being guarded by, and snuggling with, a furry friend.

Best friends, animal style

Nonhuman species have connected with each other in strange and wonderful friendships, too. You may have heard about the baby hippo that cuddled up to an elderly tortoise in Kenya after being orphaned by a tsunami. How about the hamster that slept in the coils of a snake in a Tokyo zoo? Or the polar bear in Churchill, Manitoba, that played with a chained sled dog? But while other animal pairs might occasionally have close bonds, none seems to rival humans in their ongoing love for other species.

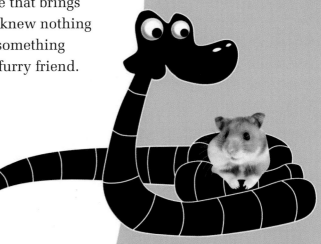

WHY do you WONDER why?

You are special and unique. And you are connected to other people and all living things all over the world, now and in the past. The things you do are puzzling at times, but they reveal your human heritage.

Hiccupping and burping, seeing and dreaming all began long, long ago. Over millions of years, your ancient ancestors developed these behaviors and passed them along to you. Your more recent human ancestors gave you the ability to cry, talk, sing and crave french fries. They also bestowed a very special trait: a large and curious brain.

Five million years ago, your prehuman ancestors had brains the size of oranges. Today, your brain has the mass of a cantaloupe. Greater brain size and complex thinking meant that early humans could invent new strategies for survival. They could ask questions, investigate problems and figure out solutions. Curiosity helped your ancestors as they moved from Africa into Europe and Asia. Much later, it propelled explorers across oceans, over mountain ranges and onto the polar ice caps. Eventually, seeking to know about other places took humans all the way to the moon.

Scientists have figured out a lot about the past. Still, many mysteries remain. It's no surprise that you wonder about things — you belong to a curious, questioning species. Now, that is truly wonderful — and totally human!

Glossary

amphibian: an animal, such as a frog or salamander, that lives both in water and on land

ancestors: relatives who lived a long time ago

arteries: small tubes that carry blood from the heart to all parts of the body

bacteria: microscopic, one-celled living things

domesticated: tamed for use by humans

dominant: stronger or more capable, such as a dominant right or left hand

family tree: a branching diagram that shows ancestors and how living things are related

generation: a group of living things that are approximately the same age

genes: the basic units of heredity. Genes, which are passed from parents to children, influence physical traits and carry instructions for cells.

hormones: chemicals that carry signals throughout the body

nerves: bundles of fibers that carry information between the brain and other parts of the body

neuron: a cell in the brain, spinal column and other parts of the nervous system

primates: a group of animals that includes monkeys, apes and both modern and prehistoric humans

reflex: an automatic action directly triggered by a particular event

species: a group of organisms that look like one another and can reproduce and have offspring

trait: a distinctive feature, such as having black hair or being a fast runner

Bye!

Index

Image credits